The Third Glass: When Drinking Becomes An Issue

The Third Glass: When Drinking Becomes An Issue

CASUAL DRINKING OR ALCOHOLISM AND HOW IT HAS TOUCHED MY LIFE.

JOHN MCELHENNEY

press of light and space

The Third Glass: When Drinking Becomes An Issue
Copyright © by John McElhenney. All Rights Reserved.

CHAPTER 1

The Trouble with Alcohol: She Likes to Drink, I Don't

DOES MY GIRLFRIEND DRINK TOO MUCH?

A couple walks into a bar. The woman says, "Saphire martini, dry." The man says, "Club soda with lime, please." [What's the punch line?] Bartender says, "Funny, when you came in here, I thought you guys were together."

My girlfriend likes a glass of wine while cooking dinner together. Is she an alcoholic?

I will admit right now I have a problem with alcohol. At times my life was out of control, and alcohol was the problem. Of course, I wasn't the one drinking, it was my dad. My entire family was held hostage by my father's drinking, his anger, and his resentment.

My brother too, eight years older than me, did quite a stint as an alcoholic. I've seen the ravages of drinking, and I've veered away from drinking in my life. Not because I'm afraid of having a problem, but because I've learned to distrust that buzzy feeling.

Today, however, she's not lonely or bored. She's saying to me that she's happier and more confident in our relationship than she can remember being at any time in her past. And still she drinks. So... there's something else at play here. Is it my problem with drinkers? Is it her wanting to drink less and still having a couple of glasses of wine a night?

It's not that my girlfriend has a drinking problem. She likes to drink. She will admit that she'd like to drink less. And she also will tell me that her drinking is more of a habit than addiction and that she used to drink out of boredom or loneliness. All of this I believe to be true.

For a while, I was worried about this disconnect between us. She drinks, she knows tons of wines she likes, she has some sort of romance with martinis and talks knowledgeably and sometimes longingly about drinking. This was beginning to trip me out.

IS MY GIRLFRIEND AN ALCOHOLIC?

Then I realized I was tripping because of MY reaction to her drinking rather than her drinking. It was my drinking problem that was causing my own fear and doubt to enter the relationship. So I talked about it.

She listened. She didn't get defensive. I didn't try to fix or change her. I didn't ask her to stop drinking.

I did want to understand more about what made her drink even when she was with me. Habit? Maybe, but that's not a good reason. Loneliness or fear? Maybe when she was living in a different house half the time. But when we were together she couldn't be lonely. So I started understanding something about her and about me. She liked to drink. And I was afraid of drinking, hers or my own. So, I was the one with the problem. Kinda.

I told her about my fear of drinking, more specifically, her drinking. "I am amazed how perfect you are, but this objection keeps popping up in my mind. I wanted to talk about it."

"Sure," she said, without a hint of frustration.

"Over margaritas, of course!"

"Of course," she joked. "Let me change clothes and we can go."

That was a few months ago, and she's still drinking. I'm even drinking a bit. Partially to join her, partially to allow me to learn from her about all of her travels, wine pairings, and knowledge of alcohol. She really is sort of an amateur-expert.

At the same time, I had to confront my own fears, and own them. It was MY fear of alcohol that was causing me trouble. And it was my hyper-vigilance against drinking that was creating the issue. So we kept dating, she kept drinking, and I kept talking and writing about it.

This was a big reveal to me: *Everyone who drinks is not an alcoholic.*

Okay, so I was letting go of that idea as I was observing our relationship and interactions around alcohol. She and I exchanged some jovial banter about her drinking and I sipped the Pinot and smiled. And over time I began to see what was bothering ME about her drinking. So I told her about my theory. Here it is.

The Third Glass (Make the choice consciously.)

The third glass of wine determines whether we are going to have an evening together or you are going to head off into some other place where I can't really reach you or relate to you. One glass to cook, one glass with dinner... and then a choice.

Towards Me (No more wine means let's be together tonight.)

If she is happy and content, I can't see why she would need that next glass of wine to feel happy or secure. If she knows and experiences my love as true and present, she wouldn't want to turn away from those feelings by dipping further into the wine. And here is my own wounded boy's idea: if she loved me, she wouldn't drink until she was intoxicated.

Away From Me ("Yes please, pour me another" means I've had a rough day, I'm feeling tired, I'd rather go to bed early.)

WHEN DRINKING BECOMES AN ISSUE IN A RELATIONSHIP

The third glass signals an intention to move away from our closeness and conversation into some altered state. Perhaps there is a numbness or release in the intoxication for her. But unwinding with a glass of wine is different when the third glass is poured and consumed and the words begin to blend together just a bit, and her jovial attitude shifts ever so slightly towards aloof and distant.

Again, this is my reaction and my emotional response to her drinking that next glass of wine. If she chooses to drink more, I tell her, it feels like you are leaving me in some ways. I can't share at the same level. I don't want to get lovey-dovey. And the real communication between us has to be put on hold until the morning. That's how it feels to me, the sober one. I can't say how it feels for you. Perhaps I am too focused, too obsessive about not drinking, and the third glass lets you unplug not only from your stressful day, but also from my intensity and earnestness.

What I really wanted to make sure I told her, as I was discovering all this stuff about me and my reaction to drinking in general, was that I didn't need her to stop drinking. I didn't even need her to limit her drinking to two glasses. What I wanted from her was to observe when she made that decision away from our closeness and into a less approachable state.

Several things I believe to be true about dealing with

someone who is buzzed. (I define this as tipsy, slurring a bit, but mostly lucid. Not drunk, but intoxicated, or impaired. In this case, by choice.)

1. Don't take on any serious subjects with them.
2. Don't talk about their drinking until the next day when they are sober. Trying to talk to someone who is drunk about drinking is a no-win situation.
3. Make sure they are safe and comfortable. And in my case, put her to bed, lovingly, and go about my evening routine without her.
4. Sex can be okay with a buzzed person, but if you're not both a bit hazy it can make for some awkward moments. And for the most part, when she's had the third glass and I have not, my desire for sex with her diminishes a bit.

So now we've had this talk. I've made up this concept of the Third Glass and she says, "I think a lot of people will really understand what you are talking about."

As we move forward, I am clear with her about my limits for me. I might have a beer or a glass of wine with dinner, but that's about it unless we go out for margaritas. And for her, the choices are a bit more complex. I'm sure I've caused her some stress around this, but it has to be out in the open and discussed.

When she has the third glass of wine, in my mind she is turning away from the relationship and into some self-imposed isolation or altered state. I have to let go of the outcome, and let go of my expectations, or speak up if I have a problem. [Again, please note, this is my frame around her drinking, not hers.] When she asks for a glass of water after dinner, she is signaling that she wants to remain close for the rest of the evening. Both choices are fine. If I don't attach my own stigma to the choice, I can allow her to take either path without guilt or shame. I can let go of my baggage and allow her to be exactly who she wants to be.

If she drinks the third glass, I begin looking for what I'm going to do that evening when she's fallen asleep. If she asks for water, my mind enters into a different set of fantasies that involve her participation. The real joy is that we've had this discussion. I even said I would run this chapter by her before I published it, so she could edit or give feedback. The last thing I want is to damage our relationship by exposing too much or causing her pain.

MY PARTNER LIKES TO DRINK, A LOT MORE THAN I DO

Last night, as I was cleaning up the dishes I looked at her with a sly grin as I held the cork above the bottle in an unspoken question. "Yes," she said, "Put the cork in the bottle and get me a glass of water." What that said to me was, "I'm here, I'm happy, and what are we going to do together tonight?"

Afterword: And the amazing thing is after I read this to her we were closer and even more ready to have the discussion at the moment about drinking, hers AND mine. (grin)

CHAPTER 2

The Third Glass Is an Anti-Aphrodisiac for Me

A WINE RACK DOES NOT AN ALCOHOLIC MAKE, A WINE LOVER DOES NOT A PROBLEM REVEAL, DRINKING IS NOT THE DEVIL'S WORK, PROHIBITION HAS NEVER SOLVED ANYTHING.

I'll admit, drinking from time to time is fun. Last night, for example, we had a round of margaritas at a nice restaurant. And the happy hour appetizers made the accidental outing more like dinner than the spontaneous happy hour it actually was. I was the driver, so I waved off the second round for me as I was nodding for my sweetheart to have another. It was a warm fuzzy of an evening at that point. All sparkle ponies and grinning selfies from the comfy couch.

We were both feeling fine when we left before the real dinner crowd arrived. We'd missed the major 5 o'clock traffic jam and arrived home in 20 minutes. In the kitchen, we discussed what movie or show we were going to watch.

"Well, I think we're going to need a short format show," I said, as she poured a glass of wine. Sure there was a moment of disappointment as I acknowledged her eventual departure, but I was okay with the idea. I had things I could do after she fell asleep.

And that's really part of the deal. If the third glass becomes routine, we will be spending a lot less quality time, lovey-dovey time in bed, a lot less deep exploration of our thoughts, aspirations, and plans. When the third glass enters the equation, I begin to clamp down on the inspired discussions about plans, hopes, and dreams. There's some pause on my part when the smooth and slippery tone enters her voice. It's cute. I'm not angry about it. I just begin to plan what else I'm going to do after she falls asleep.

The night before, she put her empty wine glass on the kitchen table, saying, "Might leave this out for a bit more." We smiled at each other as we did the dishes and generally cleaned up the kitchen together.

As we were down to the finishing bits I picked up the empty wine glass and said, "Would you like me to wash this?" I smiled. I was not being passive aggressive; she knew exactly what I was asking. She picked up the glass, smiled at me and proceeded to fill it with ice chips. Both options were still available to her. She poured the glass full of bubbly water. A new smile crossed her face. The smile that acknowledged that she would rather stay close, connected, and beside me for the night.

"Because I'm fine either way," I said before she had decided. "It's just that if you're going to have another one you'll probably be pretty sleepy. Maybe we'll skip the show altogether."

Her decision was towards me. Later in bed, we talked a bit more about it.

"I hope my hint wasn't too over the top or irritating to you," I said.

"No, it's good. I want to stay close. You're a good influence on me."

"I just don't want you to miss a minute of this life between us. I'm so enthralled and in love that any distraction takes me away from being 100% aware and present for you."

"I don't want to miss any of you either."

"So I didn't hurt your feelings?" I asked, reaching out to take her hand. I wanted to get this moment crystal clear between us.

"Nope," she said. "I want to be able to remember

these great moments too. I want to be present for the love we're sharing at all times."

"Well, not all times," I said. "It's okay to imbibe a bit. It's even okay to go for glass four and five if that's what you want to do."

"I like that you don't really drink that much. It makes me more conscious of my drinking. And I know less is better for me, and better for us to stay close."

I took her in my arms and kissed her deeply. "There isn't enough time in the rest of our days together for me to tell you and show you how much I love you. I'm going to express it as often as I can, and the more you receive the more we both grow."

It's hard, sometimes, being the light drinker. I occasionally feel sorry for myself, wishing I had an easier way to eliminate the drinks for the evening. It has crossed my mind at various times to make some demands, to set a challenge in place, but that's also my child of an alcoholic talking, rather than a compassionate and loving partner.

Let me get this straight. She's not an alcoholic. She likes to drink. Occasionally she likes to drink more than she likes to be with me. Together, when we are drinking, there's a warm fuzzy glow. Most of the time, I turn back to water and clarity of purpose so I can get on with some of my aspirations. I don't ever aspire to have a hangover, and that's enough for me. A buzz is fun. Intoxication is not. For me.

The navigation and negotiation around drinking or

not drinking are ongoing in many relationships. Often it's a struggle within an individual to make the choice away from that third glass. But my dry-drunk mentality is no healthier than the alcoholic's. I am in my own fantasy/nightmare that has very little to do with her and her third or fourth glass.

Had I allowed the knee-jerk asshole to pass judgment on her and *any* drinking, I could've easily passed on the love of my life. I believe we have a lasting partnership. I also know we'll have plenty future conversations about drinking, not drinking, wine or beer, or in my case, more often than not, bubbly water.

Our worlds have collided and in some ways merged. For the better. I'm enjoying a bit more downtime. She's enjoying a bit more ON time as we head into the evening's entertainment with the clarity of focus and intention. And then we can reverse the mode as well. Alcohol is certainly not the only inebriant. Stress, lack of sleep, lack of healthy food all produce altered states of mental health. Even a sleeping pill I love has the potential to give me a buzz rather than kicking off a good night's sleep when I've had a bit too much afternoon coffee.

We are on this journey together. She is open to my questions and suggestions and desire for her to be more present when we make love, for example. She is okay with dancing her dance and meeting me halfway in the discussion about what WE want. **The relationship is not all about me. The balance is about how we dance through all of the issues we face.** She confronted and accepted my depressive episode. She laughed and applauded my recent job loss from the mean dysfunctional corporate gig.

Here we are.

I may cross over to the realm of the third glass and beyond from time to time when we don't have to drive anywhere. But the choice to head towards less consciousness on a regular basis is a conscious choice, nonetheless. Decide consciously when you are about to fill up your third glass. Talk about the evening with your significant other. If your plans have different trajectories, don't judge or complain. Take responsibility to say what you want and what makes you happy. Every night is a new conversation. Less and less about alcohol.

We're just beginning our journey together. I cannot assume my ideas are correct and hers are flawed. She is not flawed or damaged. She is strong and leaning into all the aspects of me. I am learning to let go of my own baggage and lean into her and all her facets as well.

The journey is marvelous and it continues.

CHAPTER 3

Drinking Fuzzy Navels and Spending Time Together Doing Nothing

> A DRINK TOGETHER SAYS, "I'M WITH YOU. I AM HERE. WE HAVE TIME."

As you become an adult, opportunities for self-regulation begin to define you. For example, if food is your thing, you might give infrequently to the call of a Big Mac and fries. And for some folks, the casual drink is the indulgence that gives them a warm fuzzy feeling. But again, as we evolve as adults, we begin to look beyond the buzz and towards other objectives.

I've been learning a lot about my relationship with alcohol in the last six months, as I've been dating, and now living with, a woman who likes to drink. And I am exploring and dissecting why *any drink* at a certain time of day feels to me like an escape, a withdrawal of some kind. Is it? Is it just me and my projections? Do I set myself above the drinkers because I abstain most of the time?

The other day, I got a chance to understand a bit of my own motivation in not drinking. My sweetie was excited about a new bottle of prosecco (Italian sparkling wine) and I have to admit it looked delicious. It was mid-afternoon on a Saturday. She casually poured two glasses and offered me one.

I didn't mean to, but in some way, I shamed her. I giggled and said, "No thank you, honey. I don't want that." I was not trying to be mean, but the giggle was an indication that something else, my own issues, was in play. In some ways, I thought she was adorable with her two flutes of champagne, and in some other region of my brain my reaction was, "What? I've still got things to do and goals to accomplish." I was at that moment contemplating a late afternoon cup of coffee. I was on my way up and somehow the offer of a cocktail felt like an invitation towards distraction, disconnection, debauchery. WAIT! What?

It wasn't that I imagined my sweetheart was a drunk or lazy or something distasteful. But it did rub me the wrong way. It made me feel superior in my denial of the diversion. Again, I was not consciously telling her she was bad, but my giggle said something else, and I wanted to look at what this was.

I was saying, "Awww, you're cute. Look at you with

your mid-afternoon cocktail. Not for MEEEEE. I've got dreams to accomplish, songs to write, posts to publish. I've got aspirations and I'm going to fuel them with caffeine, not alcohol." WOOHOO! But the message was clear, even if unspoken. "I'm better than you for not drinking. I'm stronger, more creative, and obviously more in control of my hedonistic impulses."

But I was telling myself a lie with this line of reasoning. I was trying to set myself above the person I loved. I was trying to prove my sobriety was a badge of honor.

POINT OF ORDER: Not drinking is not heroic or valiant. Not drinking is a choice.

Okay, when I started trying to look beneath my bravado and self-congratulatory shaming, I wanted to understand what the disconnect was for me as this beautiful and caring woman offered me an invitation to enjoy a tasty beverage with her.

A few weeks ago, we were vacationing in New York City and spending our afternoons exploring the city on foot. And as we traipsed around the city, I noticed how my attitude about drinking together was different. In New York, "on vacation," I allowed my own self-judging, self-regulating attitude to relax a bit. A cocktail in the afternoon on vacation might lead to lovemaking and a nap. DELICIOUS.

One evening as we were chilling in the hotel restaurant/bar I suggested tequila shots. (Tequila tends to have some kind of inhibition release for both of us, and it was Saturday night, and we were in New York City, on a vacation we'd planned for months.)

The tequila shots were delicious. And as I went back to get my truffle oil fries, I swung by the bar and got us another round. Something in me was enthusiastic about the alcohol and the warm rush of tequila fairies around my chest and neck.

Two things seem to be illuminated by these different situations and approaches to drinking with my sweet woman.

1. For me, alcohol is an occasional release, a flight into fuzzy navels and potential escape. As a joining activity, the flood of joy and warmth is as intoxicating as the alcohol itself.
2. A drink together is a way of slowing the world down, letting go of dreams and expectations of the evening, or afternoon, and allowing the infusion of alcohol and proximity to draw you closer.

When I am still mapping out options and ideas for the evening or late afternoon, a drink is almost comical to me. It laughs at the poems and songs I want to write and says, "Ah, come sail away with me."

Sometimes that is exactly what is called for in life and in a close relationship. Let go. Let yourself be intoxicated and alone with another person. And while a drink is not required for these feelings to be expressed, the liquid lubrication can loosen expressions of both concern and adoration in a non-threatening way.

For me, if that decision came daily... "Hm, is it beer-thirty yet?" I think I would constantly be trying to make a choice about "being creative" or "being buzzed." I have taken a good portion of my life and growing up to get my impulsive nature under control. For example, ice cream might be my kryptonite, but I don't have to eat it just because it's in the fridge. Today, I don't plan out my day by deciding if and when I'm going to have ice cream. I don't think that much about it. (Disclosure: if there is some tasty ice cream in the fridge, I may crave it at all times of the day, but I don't act on those cravings.) If alcohol had the same craving for me, I'd have to work a lot harder not to have it around, and not to set my objectives and quitting time by when I could have my first cocktail.

Step 1 is allowing my sweet woman to manage her own life, her own afternoons, and her own creative, loving, inspirational trajectory. And my goal is not to put expectations on her for what we are doing "later tonight" unless I explicitly make plans with her. Since we are together now, so often, it can be easy to just assume we will be connecting and snuggling every single evening, even when that isn't feasible or desirable.

Still, something in me feels a pinch of sadness when she waxes poetically about a new malbec in the middle of the afternoon. My options are to smile and say nothing. To offer up plans that might point us both in a different direction. Or, releasing my own self-judgment and joining her in a celebration of a day well spent and "beer-thirty" and "let's see where this night takes us, together, no matter what we do."

It seems to me, some of my resistance (and even repulsion) to alcohol is its ability to blunt my senses, to make me a bit more relaxed than I am without it, and to signal an end to my productive, obsessive, always-on, creative narrator. When I was younger I never wanted to miss a detail. I'm still a bit obsessed by being clear-headed and creative at all times. I don't want to miss an opportunity to illuminate some detail of my past or future life.

Currently, my sweetheart and I sail along together. I am learning to say what I want, what my intention is for the afternoon (on a Saturday, for example) and thus set some expectations for her of how I would and would not like to interact. I can only assume that when I suggest drinks it lubricates a fond and familiar togetherness for both of us. I am learning to embrace this idea and indulgence of time and attention.

POINT OF ORDER: A cocktail together cordons off a bit of time where your focus can be exclusively on the other person and the joy of simply being together.

A drink together says, "I'm with you. I am here. We have time. Let's set off into the sunset and see where this journey takes us."

Setting aside time to be with another person is a special thing. Allowing that time to have no agenda and no expectations is yet another level of joy and togetherness. For me, a drink can enhance the joy or dull the prospects of the follow-on activity. The choice is more about perspective than what is right or wrong. Navigating a relationship is about expressing your desires and expectations and not letting unspoken agreements or disagreements cause resentment. Love is the number one thing. Time is the recipe. Stirring in coffee or tequila can have a radically different effect on the course of the evening.

Do I always wish that she would go for a cup of coffee rather than a glass of wine? No. Do I always have some twinge of pain when she pours another glass of wine? No. Am I learning what my relationship to alcohol looks like? Yes. Do I have the answers? Hell no.

Onward and upward, together.

CHAPTER 4

The Little Oblivion I Seek

I have to admit I do appreciate a minor amount of intoxication. I don't do it often, but when I do, I revel in the relaxation, the joy, the fun of cutting loose. But that's a little different from oblivion. When we seek oblivion, we are looking to escape something, to get away from the complexities of life or living or love or loss. I understand this. Sometimes I'm bored; I want to be entertained for an hour or so, and then I just want to blackout into sleep. Well, not *blackout* blackout, but you get what I'm talking about. I think at times we all want a little oblivion.

For me, when I was suffering from depression over the holidays that oblivion came in the form of a very comforting sleep medication. Ambien. No matter how rotten I was feeling, I could count on a good night's sleep when I took my little pink generic. And at $15 for a month's supply, what's to stop me, right?

Turns out while I did need help sleeping for a few nights, when my love of the sleep became something I looked forward to each day, that was a different desire right there. I was no longer having trouble sleeping, I was looking for the warm fuzzy of sleep. The big black blanket of pharma-enhanced sleep is what I was craving as an escape from the hard times.

I joked with my therapist that I was managing my life between Ambien doses. That's funny, but it wasn't very far from the truth. See, if you don't go straight to sleep, Ambien can make you a bit euphoric. And when you are depressed, a tiny sliver of euphoria can go a long way towards making you hopeful about joy in your life once again.

Each morning I would wake up a little more depressed, as I started slipping into a dark period, rather than a minor setback. And each night I would gladly affirm to my girlfriend that I'd taken my "sleepy meds."

But it was no longer about sleep. On Month 2 it was about joy. It was about a moment of feeling good and then a long dark and dreamless sleep. And they say Ambien is not habit forming. Who are they trying to kid?

I'm certain this is what many people are trying to do with daily alcohol consumption. A little buzz and a good night's sleep. But this form of self-medication is no better than my Ambien habit and probably more destructive to their health. Ambien does give you restful sleep. Alcohol actually interrupts your REM cycles and gives you poor quality sleep. So if you're drinking to help yourself get sleepy, you might consult your doctor and try something else.

But I get it. I was getting into my little oblivion moments even as my life felt like it was spinning into the pits of blackness. I was drawing ever-darkening pictures of my future in my mind. And each night I would release those wicked pains for a few minutes before I drifted to sleep. I'm guessing this is not unlike an opium habit, though I've never done opium.

Something, however, was not healthy about what I was doing. I wasn't clear about it until my prescription ran out one day in December and I missed a dose and missed my little high before falling asleep. The next day I had a much more hopeful outlook. I noted my desire to have an outreach conversation with my manager at work. I said to myself, that afternoon, "Wow, that was pretty hopeful."

The Ambien was having some sort of suppressive effect on my hopefulness. I had seen this a few years ago. I loved my Ambien sleeps, but I noted that I loved them a bit too much. And the couple nights I didn't fall directly asleep... Well, I really enjoyed those moments.

I watched my mood the next day after I refilled the Ambien. While I didn't notice a downer, I also didn't notice the lift I had felt when not on Ambien. So I took a break. And you know what? My hope came back almost like clockwork. I haven't had an Ambien since. Now, I'm not saying Ambien is bad stuff. In fact, in talking with my meds doctor about my experience, he said, "It's a useful tool when the sleep is the real risk for you. When you are getting enough sleep, it might be best for you to stop the medication."

Easy for him to say.

I longed for that happy moment. I felt like I was having no happy moments. My little oblivion felt like a reward or a respite from the depression. And it was not the first time I contemplated daytime Ambien use. (BAD IDEA. Google it, it's a thing, but it's a bad thing.)

It seemed to me if they could make an anti-depressant that worked a little bit like Ambien... But what Ambien does is release some of your natural inhibitions. In my case this gave me the feeling that I could accomplish something. It gave me momentary breaks from my hopelessness. I believed joy was returning to my life. But the dawn would often bring back the same panic and dread.

They say Ambien makes people do stuff they don't remember doing. Like eating at night, driving their car somewhere, or sleepwalking. I never had that experience, but I sure had some emails I wish I hadn't sent. Emails where I gushed on about how I was feeling better and would get my shit in order right away... In fact, why don't we meet up for coffee in the morning?

Oh, the coffee never came. But I was clearly "drunk" on something.

If drinking is a little like Ambien, I do understand the

draw towards daily drinking. It's not for me either, never has been, but daily Ambien, I could see how I might enjoy that if not for the side effects that it kills my hopeful attitude the next day and has me making promises my emotional state won't let me fulfill.

I still sort of want an Ambien at night. I'd love to get that kind of sleep naturally. But you know what? It might just be the dreams that bring back the brain's hopefulness in me. Waking up in the middle of the night to snuggle closer to my loved one, that keeps me a bit more centered. I'm not heading to oblivion each night, but I'm not waking up in hopeless hell, either.

CHAPTER 5

Going for Eleven! My Aspirational Addiction

This morning has followed my typical routine. I've had my two cups of coffee and a small bowl of yogurt. I got plenty of sleep last night. And generally, things are fine. But I want Uber-Fine! I want Rocket-Fuel-Fine! I want my third cup of coffee. *[brief pause while I brew up a cup of decaf.]*

But I'm not going to have my third cup and here's why.

- My enthusiasm will become overpowering.
- I will miss the nuance in most conversations since I'm planning rather than listening.
- I will shoot for the moon and be exhausted by noon.
- The warm fuzzies may become the cold

jitters.

That does not prevent me from WANTING the third cup, but I see the benefit of staying feet-on-the-ground real and having decaf instead. *[BTW: this decaf with a little organic coconut oil is delicious, and my body doesn't know it's 98% caffeine free.]* I'm going to have to deal with the normal problems of a normal day with non-heroic energy and strength. The third glass (coffee or wine) is a reach for something other than what is real.

For me, coffee is more of a draw than wine because I often am hoping to fire up the creative juices rather than shut them down. But wine is also a draw as the day winds down and I'm contemplating more coffee, so I can create more during the evening, or wine, so I can unplug and get to sleep, unaided, at a reasonable hour. Of course, some of my greatest creations were born of insomnia, so... Every now and then I go for the full-caffeine past 2:00 pm and I hope for inspiration.

The thing about wine, for me, is it loosens up some parts of my inhibition. Now, in reality, I need to learn to loosen those worries, anxieties, stresses without alcohol, but a single glass of wine does the trick nicely. If I'm going for escape, for me, the second glass is all I need to trend towards bed rather than the writing desk. Usually, I'm in the mood for the writing desk. It's what I do for fun as well as for money. *[Well, more on that later.]* It's what I do for entertainment, at this point.

The wine tends to release some inhibitions and

stress while giving me a somewhat blunted view of reality. That's okay. And on Saturday night, it's a perfect time to unplug the laptop and kick back for some SNL or House of Cards. No problem. But during the course of my normal weekly routine, there are very few evenings where I choose to disconnect rather than remain lucid. I don't want to miss a minute of this wonderful life, and alcohol takes some of my observational acuity away.

Back to the racy side of the third glass. This morning, the third cup lacks the rocket fuel I was hoping for while giving me the comfort of another warm and tasty beverage. Still, I want something more. I want some creative burst of energy to unhinge my morning, set me alight, get me going. Alas, I think I am stuck with my normal routine and my normal, earthbound self, to tap through this chapter and get on to my day job at the factory.

The third glass for me ALWAYS sounds like a great idea. My brain and my heart want that extra boost. My spirit and mind know that it's not such a great idea for me. Sometimes, sure, but often, no. I need my powers of observation and wit to be sharp and pointed. Anything that blunts or amps-up those powers is not serving me in the long run. So, I'll sip my decaf this morning and dream of the stratosphere, but I'll remain here in my seat with typical human powers.

CHAPTER 6

Drinking Lessons

I have had a love-hate relationship with alcohol since I was five years old. My dad was a mean drunk. I could've easily gone that direction in my life. I was a very angry young man in high school. And when I discovered (underage) drinking, I went after it with a passion. I liked how confident it made me feel. Invincible. I was in love.

The summer after my high school graduation I was at a party that had kegs of beer. I remember it being a euphoric night. I was popular and well-liked in high school, and the beer just made our joyous celebration that much more joyous. That was probably the last time I really enjoyed going beyond a light buzz. That night as I was drunk driving home, I crashed my car trying to miss a deer standing in the road. I'm amazed that I'm sitting here, after the wreck that should've killed me. I suffered a minor concussion and a lost car and that was about it. But

I woke up. I no longer thought alcohol was a great friend.

And it's not that I didn't drink after then; I drank a little bit and still enjoyed the feeling of being slightly buzzed. I'm sure in college I also drank to excess and had a few wicked hangovers. But it was never the same after my wreck. I saw the physical danger of being drunk. It was about that time, during my second year in college, that my dad got sick.

Now, the really amazing part of this new development was that my dad could no longer drink because of the meds he was put on. As he sobered up from 20 or 30 years of constant drinking, he sort of became my dad for the first time. At 19 I was able to relate to him in a new way. When he wasn't drinking, his old happy-self came back. Sure, there was a ton of sadness, because he was dying of brain cancer, but we had time. I got my dad back, for about a year and a half before he died. And although the drinking didn't directly kill him, the drinking had kept him hidden and distant from me for most of my formative childhood.

If I had some doubts about the coolness of alcohol up until that point, I got the message loud and clear. Drinking sort of fucked up your thinking. And continuous drinking changed the physical/chemical structure of the brain. It was a heavy price for ending the estrangement between my father and his kids, but it was the best (and worst) time I'd ever had with him. While he was dying. We reached for each other and sought time that we could be together for the first time in my life.

I don't know that I've ever been drunk since my dad died. What's the point? It's an escape. I was focused on capturing and recording my life (through writing and other creative projects) and didn't want to miss a minute of it being fogged up by drinking. That's not to say I didn't want to from time to time. But something held me back. Some internal governor was set, and after two beers I was done. I still like the taste of some beers. But I usually have something I'm working on in my creative brain that I don't want to lose to the buzz, so I just don't drink that much. And as a preference, I'd rather have sparkling water.

But that doesn't mean I haven't continually been touched by alcohol. I just choose to stay conscious. I hope that I am facing my issues head-on rather than trying to escape from them or block them out. I have issues. But I'd rather face them sober.

CHAPTER 7

Drinking Is Not the Problem: It's the Emotional Exit that Wrecks Relationships

I've had several relationships where alcohol became the third lover in a sick *ménage à trois*. Where the bottle began to compete for my attention. And it's not that alcohol is my trigger, it's that alcohol abuse is a warning sign that spells more trouble than you can imagine. If you drink, do so with respect and moderation. If you drink a lot, make a note of how this behavior might be affecting the loved ones around you. If you are in a primary relationship with a non-drinker and you drink to excess, know that there is a major disconnect between you at that moment you are feeling so buzzed. A drunk person cannot relate to a sober person. And a sober person can often feel like a threat to the drinker and the drinker's friends.

My dad was a heavy drinker, as was my dad's mom. My dad's dad was a teetotaler. As my dad began to drink more in his adult life, he began spending more time with his mom, drinking, and less time with his young family. It was a problem. It became the problem that cost my dad everything. It cost me my dad. I'm not a fan.

But I'm not against alcohol consumption. I have several bottles of wine in a rack in my house and several more bottles of beer in my fridge. I can't tell you anything about the beer in the fridge, as it was left behind by my "game night" friends last month. Eventually, I will get around to drinking the beer. And someday, the six bottles of wine will be consumed. I'm not sure when. I don't really drink much.

I have been in relationships where drinking was more a part of our fabric. I was more of a drinker in college, and I recall many a buzzed afternoon on my roof deck enjoying some summer rum punch. Today, that sounds awful, not because I don't like a buzz every now and then, but because I have a lot I want to accomplish in the next 50-or-so years of my life, and alcohol slows me down, numbs me up, and makes me lazy. I could envision a tasty rum punch on my back porch with my girlfriend, but it's not going to happen until the temperatures get lower than the surface of Mars.

I'd like to focus for a second on what the non-drinker

goes through in response to someone, a loved one, starting to check out of reality by consuming alcohol. (Yes, for this entire series you can substitute any addiction for alcohol: meth, tobacco, pot, running, skydiving.) It is my experience that I'm most interested in. At one point, I thought I could be in a relationship with a drinker by maintaining my own boundaries and my own program of recovery. But I was wrong about several aspects of the equation.

- A drunk person is not having a relationship with anyone (they are escaping a relationship, even with themselves).
- A sober person, as much as they love the drunk person, cannot make sense of why their loved one would choose alcohol over a highly-aware evening with them.
- A lopsided relationship with alcohol will cause problems, no matter how evolved or committed either partner is.
- Only the drinking partner knows what's going on in their lives.
- Only the drinking partner can make a change in their lifestyle, just as only they can decide to have or not have that next glass of wine.

I was going to Al-Anon as part of my healthy living strategy. Al-Anons often do not have a substance addiction problem, we have an emotional addiction problem. As a drinker is addicted to drinking, an Al-Anon is addicted to feeling the feelings. And sometimes, those feelings are unhealthy, unproductive, and can be outright destructive. But we're somehow led to believe that "feeling the feelings" is the height of mental health. That idea is old. That idea is wrong. And I'm going to show you that your feelings are not always real, and they are not always worth paying attention to.

CHAPTER 8

The Sober Person's Perspective in a Drinking World

Fuck the Feelings

As the sober person in a relationship with a drinker, you go through a lot of mental gymnastics trying to make sense of what is happening. Rationalizations. "If I do this, they will slow down their drinking," you think. For me, it was all the damn time. I was happy, optimistic, and hopeful. Every night, the person came home and announced, "Cocktail time!" I would join in for a beer or a hard cider. And our rejoining would begin. "How was your day? Tell me about it. Here's what happened to me."

As an Al-Anon, I was always a great listener. I was listening for the solution. I was listening for how to fix the drinker. Of course, I've learned, it's not about them. It's not even really about drinking. The problem is about me. Yep, that's the first lesson of Al-Anon.

The problem is not the drinker. The problem is my reaction to the drinker.

Okay, so as I sobered up from the emotional aftermath of losing a most-beautiful partner, who happened to drink, I began to hear the wisdom of the 12-Step Program. As an Al-Anon, we apply the same 12 steps, but they are not about staying sober, they are about remaining focused on our own shit and keeping our judgment to ourselves. The drinker is not the problem. Our reaction to the drinker is the only thing we can control. It wasn't that my partner had a drinking problem, it was that I had a problem with my partner's drinking. Simple. Elegant. And hard as hell to believe, and harder still to practice in my own life.

She was not the problem. I was the problem.

How Feelings Are My Drug of Choice

I don't think you can abuse feelings like you can abuse a substance. But I don't think I'm any more sober than an actively-drinking alcoholic. I'm just addicted to something else. I feel the feels. Sometimes I get depressed and feel the feels to the point that I can't function properly. When I'm actively seeking my own recovery, I get help. I talk to a counselor. And if things get really bad, I seek out medications that can help with the chemistry mix in my mind.

But it's not the chemistry. And it's not the drinker. It's me. My focus on the feelings is the problem. I'm addicted to feelings. I'm addicted to drama, depression, manic-highs, and a whole range of other "heightened" emotional states. It's what I learned. It's how I escaped as a kid. I had several defense mechanisms as a child. As my dad drank and raged and yelled, I had a few ways to deal with the feelings of terror that welled up inside my seven-year-old body.

- I could run outside and hide.
- I could detach my mind from my body and escape into some inner world of blackness, silence, death, depression.
- I could drink/drug/run wildly into the night (of course, this option was not open until I was 15 or so).
- I could try and address the screaming parent.
- I could die.

This is the formula for depression in a child. As my dad had all the money in the world, my little family life was a living hell from the time I was about three or four. As my dad drank and got violent, I got more detached. Or I got more hyper-focused on being the entertainer of the family. They call it the hero-child.

I did good in school from elementary grades on. I

played sports. I courted the girls from first grade on. And I tried everything I could to escape my life in the house of rage and whiskey. I learned 2,000 ways to escape myself, escape my feelings, escape my depression. Some of that looked like a hyper-expressive kid with lots of energy and lots of ideas. A "flight of ideas" they call it in psychiatric terms. Or "delusions of grandeur." I was certain that my behavior, in some magic way, was going to save my father from his alcoholism. Through my magic tricks (I was a professional magician by fourth grade) or my touchdowns (I was a star Pop-Warner running back, from second grade on).

But of course, none of my tricks and disappearing acts worked to diffuse or rescue my home life. The rest of my youth I spent trying in some way to rescue my father from his spiraling death dance with the bottle. He was not a pretty drunk. And he made it very hard to even contemplate a relationship between us. I remember being in seventh and eighth grade, and my dad would call me on the phone, drunk, and yell horrible things at me about how I didn't love him.

MY DAD DID NOT WILLINGLY SOBER UP

When I was 19 my dad was diagnosed with brain cancer. The drugs they begin injecting into him made it impossible for him to continue drinking. It simply made him vomit. There was no escape for him, at least not through the bottle. His escape would only be provided by death. And he rushed, terrified, towards that fate, over the last 18 months of his life, as he rose and fell between periods of remission and utter blackout sickness. The cancer was a bitch. It took his life at the very young age of 55. But my dad was gone a lot earlier than that.

From the sober side of that relationship, it was my understanding that my father was not himself from the time I was about 10 (when the Cutty Sark flowed with a vengeance) to the moment when chemo sobered him up. It was a car crash of an abstinence program. And I'm sure the withdrawals were mixing with his chemo as he stumbled through his own personal darkness. He was dying and he knew it. He clung to life. But at the same time, he was madder than hell. He cursed his fate. He cursed his bad luck. He cursed the fact that he couldn't drink, and his young wife could.

Over the course of my dad's battle with cancer, we repaired our father/son relationship as best we could. There simply was not enough time. We missed each other. We longed for a better connection. We strived to understand one another. But he was facing the great wide maw of death. And his emotions were all over the map. He was still rageful, but at God. He was loving and gentle, perhaps, like he had been when I was a young child. And for a good part of it, he was a dad who just wanted more time with his kids.

My two sisters moved back to Austin, Texas as my dad went into treatment for his cancer. We all rallied. He died anyway. And we were all devastated. But none as devastated as my father, who sat in his hospital bed and cursed and cried at God who was robbing him of the rest of his life.

In the end, my father, the most important man in my life, curled up in that hospital bed and became childlike and tiny. His body, when he died, weighed less than 80 pounds. As a fully-functional alcoholic, my dad weighed 250 pounds and had a huge potbelly. The little bird-of-a-man in the hospital bed still had the paunch, but he looked a lot like the starving Indians we see on the charitable-donation porn that's on television just before Christmas.

I cried at his bedside every afternoon after my college classes let out. I stayed in the hospital, beside my dying tiny-birdlike-dad, until he finally flew away and escaped his tortured body and tortured life. But I've never forgotten the alcoholic trajectory that got us there. I'll never forgive my dad for choosing the bottle over me. He did. He regretted it as he was dying and grasping to find his love for me, for us. And I'll never forget the fear and anger in his eyes as the cancer finally took his ability to speak. He eyes in that hospital room with a breathtaking view of the University of Texas, where I was a drowning student, said everything.

- God don't let me die like this.
- God, why have you forsaken me?
- God, I love my kids, I love my life, I love my newly found Jesus Christ, why are you still killing me?
- God, I'm not ready to die yet. Can you give me more time? Can you give me back my "good years" for a few more years?

I wasn't there when my dad passed. His sister said

it was peaceful. I cried that entire summer. I almost failed out of the university. And I hit a depressing low that could've killed me too.

I didn't kill myself. I didn't turn to alcohol, or cocaine, or fast cars. I struggled. But I struggled stone-cold-sober. And I've pretty much lived my life in a sober manner ever since. Sure, I did a stint with drinking and drugging in high school and early college. But as I continued to get healthier, as I climbed out of a debilitating depression back into the land of the living, I learned to manage my own recovery. I got involved with Al-Anon. And I sobered up from my emotional addiction. I've been in recovery ever since.

That's my Father's Day memory. A dying dad, a striving son, and our inability to form a healthy relationship. By the time we reconnected, I was 19 and he was dying. We did our best. I spent as much time with him as I could. And we cried together. I rode in his golf cart as he golfed.

I forgive my father for his alcoholism. I don't forgive alcoholism. And in my adult life, I can't maintain a relationship (romantic or professional) with someone who drinks heavily. It's not good for me. And I certainly can't be in a relationship with a "drinker." It won't work out. I'll just get depressed again trying to get them to stop drinking. It's between me and my higher power. I'm choosing sobriety in all my relationships. Even with God, I'm going to maintain a clarity that comes from drinking bubbly water rather than bubbly.

May you find your own path with or without alcohol.

But be aware, alcoholism is a baffling and cunning disease.

[I love you, Dad. And I miss you every day.]

CHAPTER 9

Why Adding Cocktails to Your Emotional Mix Might Not Be Working

> A cocktail at the end of a rough day is an understandable indulgence. If it becomes routine, you might be trying to cope with parts of your life that are out of balance.

Alcohol is a depressant. It dulls feelings and muddies our thinking. Sure, a celebration with drinks might feel exhilarating, and that's the idea, but it also might be robbing you of some of the good feelings in addition to making your recollection of the event less sharp. That is usually some of the effect regular drinkers are seeking. The goal might be stated as "relaxation," but the underlying issue could very well be unresolved feelings of anger or sadness. Sure, you might just love the taste of wine, but if you're seeking the comfort of a bottle nightly, you might want to look at some of the other things in your life. Perhaps you are avoiding some underlying issues.

Several times in my life alcohol has played a role in my own avoidance.

In high school, for example, when my father was accelerating his own demise with alcohol, I took to drinking for entertainment and escape. It was the early '80s so there was a bit of pot going around our school as well. Sex, drugs, and rock 'n roll, without much sex. But we took to our recreational drinking with gusto. I recall an afternoon, my senior year, a few weeks before graduation. The spring weather had released all the budding trees and cool breezes and a group of my friends decided to skip school on a Friday and meet at my father's house. He was at work and his wife was traveling, so we had his large house and swimming pool to ourselves. And his liquor closet. By the end of the afternoon, we decided it would be cool to climb the radio/TV tower behind his house. Drunk and stoned, we climbed about a quarter of the way up the rickety, swaying tower. We were happy, high, and stupid. Fortunately, on this journey, nobody was hurt. I still see one of the guys from time to time and we both still remember the vivid afternoon of debauchery. It was a memorable buzz and a celebration of our closing high school career. It was also a way of self-medicating my depression about my father's drinking.

As the year came to a close, one of my friends had a graduation party with an open keg of beer. I'm not sure how the parents were not informed. I believe at that time you had to give a driver's license or credit card as a deposit for the keg. It was a beautiful party. Great weather. We were all feeling high and getting buzzed. I left the party feeling bulletproof and optimistic. Euphorically optimistic. Halfway home, a deer decided to walk across the road in front of me. I was driving too fast. I swerved to miss the deer and flipped my car off the road into a ditch. The real magic trick was how I missed the huge oak on one side and the deeper (100 foot) ravine on the other side. I flew off the road and busted the driver's side window out with my head. A nearby neighbor heard the ruckus and came to investigate. He drove me home. I don't remember any of it past the deer entering the road in front of me and my tires starting to squeal as I jerked the wheel.

I was very close to death at that point in my young life, and alcohol had played a huge part in my anger, depression, and overwhelm. After my wreck, I began to see drinking in a different light. I experimented with drinking a bit more in college, nearly earning my first DWI on the way home from a bar. But I never had the same enthusiasm for beer after that. And over the course of my college life, I started giving up drinking altogether. I saw how it made my friends and girlfriends into blabbering fools. And when you're not drinking, drinking people become fairly unattractive.

Now, as I've traveled through two marriages and a handful of long-term relationships, my curiosity about drinking and my epiphanies around fancy gin drinks have waned. I'll still have a margarita from time to time, but it's a rare event. When I open my fridge, I'm most likely to go for a bubbly water over anything else. It is merely a choice. I choose to remain sober and clear. Drinking makes me a bit lethargic and less motivated. In the course of a work day, I've often still got creative projects I want to work on after dinner, for example. One beer with dinner might be okay, but it's more likely to lead me to an early bedtime or zoning out on a TV show. Again, it's fine, from time to time, but it's not my initial choice. And, in fact, it's becoming more of an aversion. Why have a glass of wine? What does that second margarita do for you?

Alcohol can be an emotional lubricant. I was married to a woman who needed a few drinks to finally express what was going on our relationship. We'd reach some odd clarity while she was buzzed and, unfortunately, she'd forget all about it in the morning. If you need alcohol to actually say what you're feeling, or ask for what you desire, you might consider working on your relationship in therapy.

The choice to drink or not to drink is a personal one. I don't condemn you for drinking, but I do ask myself as the third glass is being poured, what is causing you to check out? When you tip over the edge of inebriation, you are slipping into an isolation that I cannot join you in. You are exiting the relationship by using alcohol to numb or loosen your feelings. I can't and won't follow you there.

I choose to remain unaltered these days. I can work on my other addictions: sugar, queso, and Frappucinos.

CHAPTER 10

Passive-Aggressive Miscommunication: Do You Want a Drink?

> "Stop trying to change me."

In my two marriages, there were plenty of power struggles. Just like in any relationship, people begin to wield influence. And asking for a change is acceptable. Manipulating the other person, through anger or rewards, in order to get them to do something you want but would rather not ask them to do, well, that's called passive aggression.

We often want different behaviors from those around us. I'd like the person in front of me to drive more quickly. I'd like my kids to pick up the towels from the bathroom floor. My role is to ask them to pick up their towels. Repeatedly. They are teenagers, they could be not doing it to piss me off or get some autonomy.

> AS ADULTS IN RELATIONSHIPS, WE NEED TO BE AWARE OF THE DIFFERENCE BETWEEN ASKING *FOR* SOMETHING AND ASKING *AROUND* SOMETHING.

Let me give you an example from a few years ago.

My girlfriend at the time liked to drink. Not a problem. I am rather "meh" about alcohol, but I could always say yes to an ice cream. So when we are approaching a bar and she asks, "Would you like a drink?" I hear that she is asking if I am thirsty.

The other night she asked me and I said no. As we got closer, she asked, "Are you sure?" "Yep," I said. And she asked a third time, "What about a water?" "Nope," I said with some frustration beginning to show in my tone, "Nothing, thank you." I probably said something like, "Quit asking." But I don't recall. I do know she reacted with a pout, letting me know my frustration had registered.

Later the next morning as we were sorting through our plans and replays, I made a discovery that excited me a bit.

"When we were heading towards the bar last night you asked me if I wanted a drink."

"Yes, and then you got all pissy."

"Wait. I just understood what was frustrating for me." She looked at me with suspended disbelief. "When you asked me if I wanted a drink, I wasn't sure if you were asking me if I was thirsty, or if you were making a request for me to join you for a drink."

"Okay."

"To me, they are completely different."

"I was asking if you were thirsty."

"Yes, but you don't have to ask me three times to see if I am thirsty. It's very possible what you were asking initially, was 'Will you have a drink with me?' But that's not what I heard."

"And if I knew you were asking me to join you for a drink, as in a request for us to share a drink together, then I can still say no, but I understand more clearly what you are asking. It seems like last night, the reason you asked three times, was because you might have been asking me to join you for a drink."

"Maybe."

"What do you think?"

"I think I was asking if you were thirsty?"

"Three times?"

"I agree, that's a bit much."

"So you understand how I got frustrated?"

"No, I just thought you were being an ass."

"But I'm never an ass on purpose. I'm an ass to register frustration, or if I'm clear, to ask you for a behavior modification."

So the passive-aggressive way to ask me to join her for a drink would've been to ask if I wanted a drink. But typically I say no to that question because a "drink" is rarely what I'm thinking of. If she EVER asks me if I wanted an ice cream, I'm guessing I'd be 100% compliant. But with alcohol, I'm more like 10%. Just not my thing.

In our relationships with others, we need to strive to ask for what we want. To complain when we don't get the results we wanted. And to make our own desires as clear as possible. Anything unspoken, or actions used to manipulate the person into doing what we want, well, that's out-of-bounds.

Speak what you want. Complain when you don't get it. And ask for a modification if it becomes a habit or pattern of disconnection.

"Do you want a drink?" is very different from "I'd like you to have a drink with me."

The first is about me. The second is about you. If you want me to have a drink with you, say it. It shouldn't matter if I have bubbly water or bubbly, unless that is also what you are asking.

The clearer we become in our communications, the clearer we can be with our intentions and disappointments. Only through this type of honest communication do we get tuned-in to one another.

CHAPTER 11

If Drinking Is an Issue in Your Relationship: Check-in with Yourself

> I HAD A PROBLEM WHEN MY GIRLFRIEND DRANK TOO MUCH.

That statement is so open-ended, it's not very helpful. How much is too much? What's MY problem with her drinking? And even if the statement is true, who cares? What I think is not very important when it comes to other people's drinking habits. However, if we are in a relationship and drinking continues to become a topic of negotiation and conflict, we both might need to take a time-out and reconsider our objections.

DAILY DRINKING, DAY DRINKING, AND IDENTIFYING MY ISSUES

When I was dating a daily drinker, I had some issues that were mine alone:

- Not everyone who drinks is an alcoholic (this is my legacy after growing up in an alcoholic home: I'm never quite clear on what is too much and what is none of my business).
- Because of my historical relationship with drinking and drinkers, I was unable to distinguish between my then-girlfriend's casual drinking and potential problem drinking.
- How I am affected, how I feel, about someone else's drinking, if we are in a relationship, becomes an issue when we don't agree about the drinking and how it might be hurting our relationship.
- I can drink and stop after one without any problems, and so could my then-girlfriend, but frequently she would not stop at Drink 3 or even Drink 4; often she would continue drinking to the point of slurred speech and impaired functioning.

And some of the issues were clearly my then-girlfriend's responsibility:

- She rarely went 24 hours without having a drink or two.

- While she was super high-functioning, her emotional availability was mostly limited to the morning and early afternoon hours.
- She once said as we were about a year into dating, "You will probably save my life, because you don't drink with me."
- When she chose to cut loose, she occasionally drank to incoherence.

IS MY GIRLFRIEND AN ALCOHOLIC?

That's not really for me to say. I am not a doctor. I am not a therapist. What I did learn over time: her drinking was taking a hefty toll on my emotional and spiritual livelihood. If your drinking is an issue in your relationship, you may have a drinking problem. AND, perhaps she did not have a drinking problem; instead, I had a problem with her drinking. That is a possibility. But the reality was, it was a problem and she was choosing not to address it, even after I began writing some blogs about the Third Glass. (She green-lit the posts.) Somehow she encouraged me to write about her potential drinking problem and yet failed to address it in terms of how it was affecting our love life.

Only the individual can determine for themselves if they drink too much or if they are an alcoholic. In our case, the alcohol became the dividing issue. Although she initiated the break-up, she continued to seek out a relationship between us, long after the drinking had become my stated issue. I had a problem with her drinking. Neither of us had a doubt about that.

But what we didn't agree on was what WE as a couple were going to do with our alcohol divide.

WHAT ABOUT DRINKING NOW?

If you drink, I'm okay with it. I will join you for a drink now and then. And I will support you in your entertainment and relaxation. But when that drinking begins to affect and damage our relationship, I'm going to speak up and ask for some modification or moderation of your behavior. And, it's okay if you say no. It will probably be the end of our relationship, but I get it: everyone has their own priorities and their own path in life.

I have not had any contact with my former drinking girlfriend for about six months. And, of course, I hope she is doing well, drinking or not drinking. Her drinking today is absolutely none of my business. When we were involved in a relationship, however, her drinking did become an issue in our relationship. She chose not to address it, and I chose to sever our connection, partially because her buzzed evenings were feeling lonely and hopeless to me.

Drink if you like. Drink within reason. And, certainly, cut loose when you want to, as long as you are not driving. But, pay attention if the drinking becomes an issue between you and your partner. At that point, you both have a decision to make.

While I drink very little, I'm beginning to appreciate a good tequila. I find this mildly humorous and ironic.

CHAPTER 12

She Was Lovely and She Liked To Drink

Given those two facts, her loveliness and her affinity for alcohol, I was not too alarmed at the start of our relationship. She was hilarious, she was highly functional, and she was a physical homage to fitness and pleasure. To say we started in the bedroom would be to miss the fact that we'd known each other for several years before we got together. But we revved up the bedroom as soon as we cleared the initial dating hurdles. And quicker than my mind or heart had a chance to register any alarm at the wine charm that formed a good part of her evening, I was in love. Or whatever you call it at the early stages of a relationship when you're crazy about someone and overlook the red flags.

HER DRINKING, MY PROBLEM

The first time I put her to bed in a slurry state was in Week 3. I sat down on her couch and contemplated my predicament.

- I could not be with an alcoholic.
- I didn't know what high-functioning alcoholism looked like.
- She was so amazing in her beauty, fitness, and humor.
- Maybe she was just tired.
- Maybe I should run for the hills.
- I didn't want to be alone.
- I was into the sex, really into it.

Later that week I talked to my therapist. He introduced me to the concept of "harm reduction." Maybe she did like to drink a bit too much. Was it harming anyone? Was my reaction to her drinking my problem or hers? What would constitute a problem? Did I have to make a decision right at this moment, either way?

I stayed in the relationship. I fell further in love with this amazing woman. And in some moments of revelry, I tried to join her in the hazy evening glow of pinots or margaritas. But it wasn't ever going to be my thing. It was definitely her thing. Still, I was open to the relationship, to staying curious about whether the drinking was an issue or just an issue for me. Well, I learned those are the same thing. If it's an issue for one of you, it's an issue. But that awareness would come later on.

JUMPING INTO THE HEART OF LOVE

Then we were in New York City, and we were talking about marriage, and we bought (she bought) rings for us at Tiffany's. And in a matter of months, I had exactly what I thought I wanted. A Relationship with a capital "R" and an energetic and enthusiastic partner. And a hopefulness about all that was ahead for us. We got engaged, we walked 12-mile-days around the city, and we committed to better or worse, in theory. We didn't set a date, but we set our intentions. "I want to spend the rest of my life with you," she said. I agreed.

BUT NOT ALL THAT GLITTERS IS GOLD

And life roared on. I passed through a few jobs. She sold a house and moved in with me. Then bought a house for us and my two kids. Within a year we seemed to be well on our way towards the marriage we had both hoped for in previous attempts. I was writing my TV pilot. She was getting promoted at work, and we were traveling around the world together, in a fantastic runway towards our eventual marriage. It was awesome.

Then my wheels came off. Right at a peak moment, as we were traveling to England for my band to play the Cavern Club, I slipped into a deep depression. I had been fired unceremoniously from my job the day before we left. My TV pilot was not getting the traction I needed to keep striving forward. And some sort of freefall hit me.

Looking back, I can now see how the alcohol issue was causing me some concerns. I had begun writing the Third Glass series of blog posts. (How ironic that she knew about and even encouraged my posts about her drinking, and yet...) But it was not her drinking that took me down. Often my depressions come after some major financial setback (divorce, job loss, ex-wife filing against me with the Attorney General's office). Somehow, in my mind, my prospects for employment were damaged, my belief in my own creative prowess (writing and music) was waning, and my relationship had a serious flaw.

We stumbled along together, but the issues only compounded.

"How can you be sad, you've got me?" she asked.

"It doesn't work that way," I tried to explain. But it's hard to explain hopelessness at the existential level to someone who thrives on positive momentum.

MAKING CRITICAL CHOICES

I don't think she is to blame for not recognizing that her drinking was hurting me. Her drinking was not the principal reason I was depressed. But there were choices being made, on both our parts, that were not towards a more healthy relationship. I was holding on for dear life. She was tolerating me, hoping I would pull out of it.

In the end, she was making a choice to turn towards the fog of drinking each night, rather than sit in the bummed-out relationship with me. It's hard to know why anyone develops a nightly drinking habit. Are they self-medicating some depression of their own that they are unable to attack head-on? Are they simply escaping the everyday grind of life? In our case, was she checking out of the damaged relationship and into her own oblivion? I don't know. And I can't begin to unravel it for her.

What I do know is that in the end, when I called to let her know I was heading off to a second date with a new woman I was interested in, she pleaded for about 30 seconds. She would quit drinking. She didn't want it to just end. But over the course of the two years we were together, we never addressed her drinking directly. We talked about it. We talked around it. I wrote about it. And perhaps I did not do enough to demand she change her intake to be more present with me. But again, I don't think it's anyone's business how to manage the other person. I made my desires known; she continued to drink. I tried to drink with her from time to time. But it was not my daily go-to activity.

THE CLOSE OF BUSINESS BETWEEN US

It was heartbreaking, stumbling through a relationship as it's coming apart. I could not pull up out of my depression. She could not figure out what she was getting from me in such a depressed state. And she chose her single-and-traveling lifestyle over being with me. But at that moment, in the end, I still loved her, still wished it had worked out for us. I still felt the dream we had written for our future. But somewhere along the path, we both turned away from the relationship and towards our previous dysfunctions. I was sad. She was drinking. And we were going our separate ways.

CHAPTER 13

Alcohol May Not Be Your Friend

ALCOHOL IS A DRUG

Let's get clear about something right upfront. Alcohol is a depressant. As you consume more alcohol, your overall systems (emotional, mental, spiritual, physical) are being suppressed. In the recreational use of alcohol, this has a slight euphoric effect. We feel a bit high with the first few drinks. But as we continue to consume this powerful drug, the fun turns sanguine. We begin suppressing the good stuff as well.

As an addictive substance, alcohol stands alone as an acceptable vice. People love to drink. Drinking = happiness, celebration, relaxation, recreation. And drinking is probably one of the most harmful habits we can acquire. As we come to rely on the euphoric properties on a more regular basis, our brains become conditioned to think that "fun" doesn't happen without the inclusion of drinks. How many of us come home from a hard day at work and "reward" ourselves with a drink? I'd guess the number is very large. And alcohol companies are working to keep their image glamorous and hyper-happy.

What I've noticed in partners who drank regularly is that alcohol became somewhat of a required additive. Friday and Saturday nights were for drinking a lot. The other days of the week were lighter drinking. But a lot of their attention and energy would go to "what are we going to drink?" Daily alcohol consumption was a given. I am a bit worried about that habit, but I have also seen people who can manage to drink regularly and be "okay."

SHE DOESN'T HAVE A PROBLEM WITH DRINKING

In my relationship with a drinking-enthusiast, I was concerned about how much she was drinking. She was not. (Actually, she was concerned about it and liked the idea that she was dating a man who "didn't drink.") My friend summed it up for me: "She doesn't have a problem with her drinking. You have a problem with her drinking." He was right. And he was also defending his own vice habits a bit.

The bottom line on your own drinking: if it's not bothering you, and you're happy with where your life and health are heading, you're good.

The bottom line on someone else's drinking: if their drinking is affecting your relationship or your respect for the other person, there IS a drinking problem, but it might only be yours.

The bottom line for couples and drinking: if the drinking is affecting the relationship, you might want to look at how to change or modify the patterns.

I don't care if you drink or you don't drink. I often choose to abstain from alcohol for various reasons. Most of the time, I don't need to be putting a depressant into my system for any reason. Other times I am triggered (or upset) by someone else's drinking. At that point it is up to me to make a request, "Would you consider not drinking at all this weekend so we can see how that goes?" Or to make a modification in our relationship agreements, "I'm happy being the designated driver, but I don't appreciate it when you get so smashed at the party."

MAKING PEACE WITH DRINKING OR NOT DRINKING

In the month of October, I'm going to abstain from drinking any alcohol. It's just for me. I'd love you to join me, but it's really not about you.

When I don't drink, I know my emotions and mood swings are natural and not caused by any ingestion of alcohol. When I don't drink, I know that my preferred beverage is bubbly water, which has zero calories, so I might drop a pound or two. When I don't drink, I'm making a statement to the world, to my friends, and to my colleagues: alcohol is not important to me.

I have recently been joking with my inner group of friends about not being "much of a drinker." The joke part is, I was going through a brief love affair with a certain tequila. I enjoyed it. I was enjoying the escape or release of the shot or two. I really enjoyed the fetish of the "let's have a shot of añejo." I was liking it a bit too much. Like I might really go for a Frappucino at any point during a given day. I did like this tequila. And I understood a tiny bit of the allure and appeal of getting "into" a drinking habit. For fun, drink. For relaxation, drink. As a reward, drink. As an aphrodisiac, drink. Okay, let's not buy any añejo, I said to myself that last few times I've been next door to the liquor store having dinner. In the same way I refrain from buying a pint of ice cream every time I go to the grocery store. Just don't do it.

In my relationship with the drinking enthusiast, I often felt she was using the alcohol to exit the emotional connection in the relationship. More likely, she was using the alcohol to numb her own emotional connection to herself; my proximity was just collateral damage. Can I have a drink just to celebrate? Sure. I also can have ice cream at birthday parties, but I don't need to bring home a half-gallon of Peppermint during the Christmas holidays, just because I like it.

Drink if you want. Don't drink if you want. But when it starts affecting our relationship, it is my responsibility (if we're in a relationship) to tell you. If we can't come to an agreement about it, perhaps it's time for us to go our separate ways. It's okay, I'm just not that much into drinking. And I'm certainly more into you than I am into getting buzzed with you. In fact, for me, often, getting buzzed is a way to checkout of the relationship, not get closer. I understand this about my past enthusiast, and I understand this about myself.

CHAPTER 14

Sexual Hunger: How Friends-with-Benefits Became a Lie for Me

> Yes, we are sexual animals. And from time to time I imagine doing the dating thing with more of a "hookup" mentality. It won't work.

I tried having an friends-with-benefits (FWB) relationship with an ex-girlfriend once. It went really well until it didn't. I recall a conversation with my mom a year ago, when I was telling her about my experiment. "I needed to see if there was still anything to the rest of the relationship," I said.

"Why would you do that?" asked my mom, who's not been in a relationship of any kind for over 40 years.

"I still had strong feelings for her. There was part of me that wanted to work it out. When you get that close to someone, living together for several years, there's a lot to it."

The part I didn't mention to my mom but was pointed out to me by a subsequent girlfriend, "Oh, you wanted to get laid."

All three of us were right.

- I did want to get laid, and my prior girlfriend had set a new benchmark for sex.
- I did still have strong feelings for this woman, and I wanted to see if they were authentic or just loneliness.
- Why in the world would I consider resetting a relationship with someone who drank every night?

As it turned out, the whimsical reunion was just that, a whimsy. We gathered a few times and discussed the parameters for our engagement. We expressed our affection, still, for one another. And then we had great sex. And then we spent the workweek sort of feeling like we were in a relationship and knowing we were not. But I always looked forward to our gatherings. I fantasized about them. I brought little treats for her. And it seemed we were both giddy when we'd reunite. It was a mutual happy-fest. Except the aim was self-gratification. There were no future plans in our plans. And that put a slight pallor of angst on the entire scene. Still, we moved forward and enjoyed what we could of each other, as best we could.

There was no future in this FWB situation. I knew I could not ultimately trust her with my heart. She knew I was actively seeking a different relationship.

They say if FWB is going to work, the relationship has to stay sex-only. It's when feelings and plans get involved that havoc ensues. We kept it on the casual side of things for a few months. I felt we were in a win-win situation. We both got physical needs met, we both got some cuddle time and some camaraderie. And then I continued to dive into the dating apps to seek my next relationship.

It got weird. We really did still care about each other beyond the physical touch. We really did like being in each other's company. We really did laugh and have fun together. And it was complicated. I kept dating and writing and going back to her for my "needs."

I was writing about trying to find the next relationship while getting my sexual needs met with another woman. That equation was all wrong. My entire soul was mixed up. I was getting certain needs met, but somehow, something beautiful had become something sort of hollow and meaningless. It wasn't that we didn't still get off on each other, it was the idea that there was no future in the process. The memories we were building were more like masturbation fantasies than meaningful connections. Something had to give.

I had three other women in my orbit who I was

engaged in conversations with. Two via online dating and one via Facebook with an old high school friend. And my FWB. In my mind, I was keeping my options open until one of the women stood up and demanded my attention. I was ready to stand in for someone who was ready for a relationship. And I was still a hungry and selfish man.

My plan was to give each of these relationships time to show up or ship out. I would stay in "research mode" until a winner was uncovered.

And the variable was the energy and motivation hidden in our sexual animal. I still had feelings for my FWB, we'd lived together and imagined a life together. And sex was still good, although the ennui was setting in as the future imaginings had to be squelched. So... as a man, as an animal, as a hungry ghost, I invited myself along on a road trip with my FWB to an event she'd been planning for months. We'd take the trip in my new car, drive down, have a fun weekend, and drive back. No strings. That was the plan.

During the eight-hour drive, we had so much fun. It was a road trip we'd driven before, in much darker times, and we were buoyant with the anticipation of the fun weekend. We got to our modernized airbnb hotel and checked in. My friend had already made plans, before I was coming along, to go have a happy hour with her local girlfriend. That was the plan, and that's what was going to happen. No problem. I was just so happy.

I recall thinking as she walked out the door that night, looking extremely beautiful, "This could work."

She never came back. Her disease kicked in, she stayed out late into the night and had to be taxied back to our hotel.

FADE TO BLACK.

I needed this blow to the top of my head to finally understand why our relationship was never going to work for me. Blow delivered. Girl #4 was removed from consideration. Even as the dreams of our potential were heating up during the drive, the curtain came down full force that night.

And as things have moved along, I'm now alone, having given Girl #1 from online dating a good shot at a relationship. I have no regrets about our experience. We jumped in, we loved deeply, we discovered we were not a perfect fit. We ended as friends. Perfect.

Except, I'm alone again.

A "friend" on Facebook, an older woman, made a remark about how I might need to spend some time alone rather than jumping into all these relationships. I politely thanked her and asked her to mind her own relationship business.

Alone, I am still somewhat of a hungry animal. I contemplate calling my recent ex more frequently than I'd like to imagine. It's a similar story to my previous relationship. Perhaps we can just get our physical needs met without worrying too much about the relationship or the future.

My heart does not work that way. Even as I was calling it FWB, I was still invested in making that relationship work, regardless of the cost. I now understand that nothing is worth that cost for me, and it has slowed me way down in terms of dating again. I want healthy, happy, and attractive. I want it all.

Yes, we are sexual animals. And from time to time I imagine doing the dating thing with more of a "hookup" mentality. It won't work. As I was still investing in my old relationship, still getting sexual needs met, I was invested in my soul. There is no separation between sex and heart for me. Sex is a spiritual adventure. Taken lightly, you may get your fill of junk food, but you're not going to be nourished.

For me FWB is bullshit. So is eating at McDonald's. I might do it from time to time, but I don't feel good about it. And, at the moment, I can't imagine wanting casual sex again. I want deep sex. I want big love. I want the real deal, and I'm willing to wait.

CHAPTER 15

Afterword: Am I Looking for a High?

If things are not working in your life, if things are too stressful, too anxiety-producing, too overwhelming, you might need to make a change. When life is out of balance, get curious about what's going on. Get curious about why you are choosing the unhealthy option when your head and heart are both saying, "This is not a great idea."

WHEN WE TAKE ACTION AGAINST OUR OWN BEST INTEREST

Self-sabotage is a common human trait. I know when I'm not doing well I often choose things that are not good for me. Ice cream, for example, is always an option, but when I start grabbing pints of Ben and Jerry's at the grocery store each week, I know I'm using the ice cream to meet some unmet needs. If I can pull apart the various elements in my life that are unsatisfying, I might be able to identify the parts of my life that are causing me to act in ways that do not serve my best interest. If I get fat from eating a lot of ice cream, my opportunities for a fit and healthy partner are going to: (a) increase, (b) decrease, or (c) who the f**k cares!

Often, for me, it's the "who the f**k cares" mode that gets me into bad habits. When I am acting out, I am out of balance with some essential part of my life. In the past, this MISS has often been my longing for a romantic relationship. But many things can push me into unhealthy behaviors. Laziness. Sadness about something from my past. Even over-enthusiasm can cause me to be destructive in my manic-like state of joy. The results are the same.

WHEN YOU ACT AGAINST YOURSELF, YOU'RE THE ONE GETTING HURT

I have a lot of "who the f**k cares" in me. I have resentments about the divorce, about my financial situation, and even about my "healthy but heavy" weight. In an odd way, I can even be resentful that my hair, at 56, is more gray than brown. We can find a ton of ways to be pissed off at the world. If only...

But, the way out of self-destructive behaviors is to understand them first, then make the changes you want to make towards building a happier and healthier life. That's what I'm learning these days.

What am I sad about? How am I acting out to aggravate or alleviate the sadness? How does drinking a Frappuccino every day give me relief from my sadness? (Let's see, sugar, caffeine, and caramel/coffee flavors, with whipped cream, please.) AThis is not the way out of my unhappiness. This is a path towards future sadness.

GETTING CURIOUS ABOUT SELF-DESTRUCTIVE BEHAVIORS

What is driving my desire for this coffee drink right now? What sadness am I feeling? Am I lonely? Bored? Horny? Am I just looking for that next level of energy and excitement, and it's a Friday morning, and I'm not feeling it? Maybe this cup of sugar fuel will do the trick!

Wait. Let's get curious...

What am I sad/mad about at this moment? Not much.

Am I bored? Not really, I'm writing and listening to music.

Am I looking for a high? Ah, yes, that's it. I'm happy. It's Friday and I have some fun planned for this evening and over the weekend, so what's my quest in seeking out a happy drink? MORE JOY! GIVE ME EVERYTHING NOW!

Okay, so let's look at what's behind that impulse to

the shoot-for-the moon even when things are going fine.

- I am stuck between jobs/roles in my life.
- I've been doing digital marketing for 20+ years.
- I've been writing a blog for seven years.
- I've been doing life coaching for two years.
- I'm ready to go next-level on this "single dad" thing.
- Steady progress is good but not very exhilarating.

Somehow, even on this lovely Friday morning, when everything is going my way, I WANT MORE.

WHEN MY NEEDS ARE NOT GETTING MET

I want to drive fast, I want to be on the silver screen, I want to be on stage at Lalapalooza. I want my books to sell and the Today Show episode they filmed to be broadcast. I want to blow up my current, happy, stable world for something more carnival-like. I want to date Ali MacGraw in 1972's The Getaway. I want to be Steve McQueen. I was 10 years old when that movie came out. I've wanted to be a movie star ever since.

Except, wait. Do I really want to be a rockstar? Am I interested in losing my privacy and putting my life up for display? Oh, wait... Um... (blushes)

Okay, so I'm going to come out with it. I'm working hard to develop a TV pilot for a show. I'm about to launch my podcast, Love on the Air. And I'm waiting for the edits from my third book, *A Good Dad's Guide to Divorce*. I do seek attention in a big way. Is it because I'm hollow or hurt inside? Perhaps in the past this was the motivation. But looking at my young crush on the right, I know in my heart I just want to be loved.

EVEN WHEN MY NEEDS ARE BEING MET

I want more.

It's this excessive impulse that can get me in trouble. If I'm always striving for more, I might be missing what's right here, right now. At the moment, I am as content and happy as I've ever been. My needs are being met. I just want more. I want the rollercoaster. I want to flirt with danger, with mania. (Okay, that last one is a stretch.)

My needs are being met. My aspirations are still being tickled. My budget is threatening to push me back behind a desk while I write, coach, blog, share, meetup, until I reach what?

Fame? I don't think so.

Financial independence for me? Yes.

Financial independence for me AND my loved ones? That's next-level shit right there. But that's what I'm after. And this morning I can say, "F**k you Salted

Caramel Frapp, I'm going a different way today. But thank you for the reminder."

WE DON'T HAVE TO CHANGE IT ALL RIGHT NOW

We may not be able to do a hard left turn and stop some obsessive or destructive behavior just by declaring our new healthy path. BUT, we can get curious every time we find we're leaning towards the Frappucinos in our life.

What am I feeling right now? I want a sweet, but I'm probably just hungry or tired. Today, I'm just ambitious. I'm in love. I'm playing a lot of tennis. And I'm doing exactly what I want today. And I still want that rocket fuel, so I can achieve escape velocity. Today, I have it all. Well, I don't have Ali MacGraw. But, I do have her memory, and the motivation that drove me as a 10-year-old boy still drives me today.

I want to be loved.

Today, I am. And today, I'm loving myself and my ambitions, and I'm still not going for the Frapp.

www.ingramcontent.com/pod-product-compliance
Lightning Source LLC
Chambersburg PA
CBHW071411080526
44587CB00017B/3245